The Punball Wizard

By Richard Pulsford

ISBN   978-1-912043-55-2 Paperback

978-1-912043-54-5 Electronic version

First published November 2021

Mobi Publishing Ltd

Chichester, UK

www.mobi-publishing.com

© Mobi Publishing Ltd 2020

Front cover design by comedian Chris 'Alf' Leworthy.

FOREWORD

As a child I was naturally drawn to the humour and jokes on TV programmes from the likes of Tommy Cooper and The Two Ronnies, and, since starting stand-up, I've loved watching the likes of Gary Delaney and Milton Jones. All have been proven excellent joke writers.

I first started doing stand-up at the Edinburgh Fringe in 2004 but it took me a few years to actually 'find my voice.' In hindsight it seems obvious what that voice was going to sound like because of the way my brain seems to be wired - I'm always listening out for puns and ways to play with words and phrases.

But it takes a good while to write your own set full of funny shortform jokes. Years in fact. So it was a whole decade and a half after first getting onto a comedy stage, in August 2019, that one of my jokes made the big list of jokes at the Edinburgh Festival Fringe (the one run by the Comedy Channel Dave). It felt like a great honour to be mentioned in the same list as one which frequently features jokes by some of my latter-day comedy heroes.

Less than 6 months later the Covid pandemic struck and gigs stopped running as comedy clubs and pubs were forced to close their doors during enforced lockdowns. Some gigs went online but they could never quite recreate the feel of the events which had previously only taken place in a 'real' setting.

Comedy festivals which were due to take place in 2020 and early 2021 were either cancelled or forced to go online. It was at best disheartening and at worst it brought much of the industry to its knees.

On a personal level, while waiting for the pandemic to run its course, this was at least an ideal opportunity to write more of those jokes. I had previously tested out new jokes on Twitter. I always used the same hashtag (not only to make it easy for my followers to find them but also so I could more objectively compare how well different jokes were doing).

I then saw a few people reminiscing about how there had once been a daily pun competition under the same hashtag. This prompted me to start up a brand new hashtag which I called #LunchPun for a daily pun competition. This started on 4th January 2021 and went out every weekday lunchtime. It was designed to encourage new writers and writing. It proved popular and grew rapidly until it was often attracting 100 new jokes each day.

My own Twitter output from this helped form the material for a new show for the time when I could go back on stage. This turned out to be in mid-July 2021, when Covid restrictions in England were finally being eased sufficiently.

It was at one of those first gigs, at the Durham Fringe, that I was approached by Carl from Mobi publishing who saw my show and suggested I should consider putting together a book of my jokes. My thanks go to Carl for the approach and the encouragement, and for guiding me through the publishing process, and to his colleague Brandon for suggesting artwork and designs (he came up with the Pepe the Cat character).

Special thanks also go to my comedian LunchPun friends: to Chris 'Alf' Leworthy for the striking cover design and his patience in accepting my numerous tweaks to the draft designs, to Paul Eggleston for coming up with some brilliant drawings, and to all the other Lunchpunners who have provided daily inspiration and an effective critique of my jokes by liking or not liking what I have put out there in the public domain.

It's been a challenge to go back over hundreds of my jokes from the past 17 years, select some of the better ones, and then to categorise them all. Along the way I've laughed at jokes I rediscovered. I hope that plenty of laughter is also elicited from you the reader.

Contents

Introduction: The Punball Wizard

A one-liner comedian certainly has their work cut out. Because their jokes are usually short and punchy, every single minute of their comedy routine can require four jokes. That means a full festival show lasting 50 minutes may require something like 200 jokes.

And that's not 200 jokes instantly thought up and then delivered. They need to be magically created in the comedian's mind, written down, honed and tested out.

Ideally that testing will take place in a number of different settings, perhaps first on Twitter and then in front of a live audience at one or more 'new material' nights, and there is inevitably further honing as part of that process.

Those jokes which meet the popularity test and make the final cut then need to be put into some sort of order. Oh, and somehow committed to memory (the jokes and the order) so the comedian finally has their next show.

Because many jokes don't make the cut that final list of 200 jokes belies the fact that a far greater number will not have made it anywhere near the show.

Many comedians aim to write and tour a whole new show ever year, so that requires going through the whole process pretty much on an ongoing basis to be able to write another 200 new jokes good enough to make it into the next year's show.

This book contains a mere 639 of what I consider to be many of my best jokes which have come out of the process described, from something close to a decade of writing and testing out material. Some of the jokes did well on Twitter and many made it into one of the solo shows I've toured. Some of the jokes didn't, because they only lend themselves to being read on the page. Others which worked well live but rely on the sound of the joke to work haven't been included.

I've categorised the jokes so they fall into some kind of logical groupings. This is intended to make it helpful to the reader as a reference but these categories have also proved insightful to me. For example I obviously know a fair bit about geography but know precious little about celeb culture, as reflected in the plentiful supply of jokes I have written about countries while there are none to be found about Big Brother, Strictly or Love Island. My excuse can be that I have been busy writing, travelling and gigging instead of watching TV! But I hope there is still a broad enough range of categories to amuse the reader.

How much truth is there in the jokes which touch on more personal subjects? It's almost mandatory to have jokes about girlfriends, ex-girlfriends, wives, ex-wives and offspring. To what degree I have drawn on personal experience in writing such jokes, I'll leave it for the reader to draw their own conclusions!

ALCOHOL & DRUGS

Alcohol

1.

My cheap wine rack is held together with cellar tape

2.

I've just arrived at a rally with my traction engine. I've got plenty of ethanol so I expect I'll be steaming all weekend.

3.

My local pub is looking to get more families with young children in during the day. I think they've set the bar quite low.

4.

I was consoling my friend in the pub, whose girlfriend had told him he was fat. I said, "Don't worry about that. Your round, mate".

5.

My mate wrote a song about an awful pub crawl we went on - I knew I wasn't going to like it from about 3 bars in.

6.

Fans are going completely mad over the vodka advert I'm shooting. Absolut scenes here.

7.

That's another one of my relatives thrown out of the pub, and not for the first time! He's my second cousin, twice removed.

8.

The EU body which oversees the fortifying of drinks with German wine is an add hock committee

9.

The most classically German drink is Gin and Teutonic

10.

Just found barbed wire in my beer. Someone's tried to spike my drink.

11.

Once upon a time, Bambi decided to try two drugs at once.
What a crack pot high deer.

12.

Police have found opiates hidden in a consignment of
candied cherries. Yes, glacé drugs!

13.

I left the monastery by mutual consent: I was
uncomfortable wearing an ill-fitting robe which kept
catching between my buttocks, and the other monks felt
uncomfortable about my bad crack habit

Animals

14.

The only world my hamster inhabits is one where everything can be nibbled. It's his fur chew all reality.

15.

Are all sheep rustlers behind baas?

16.

Maybe I wasted the day animal-spotting in the park, as all I saw was a single female red deer. Still, hind sight can be a wonderful thing.

17.

I've heard that matadors are puzzled as to why spectators no longer support them, and are looking for applause a bull explanation

18.

I can hear sheep being rounded up and driven off, but it's autumn so I'm not surprised to hear the sound of rustling

19.

Our newly-hatched lizard is watching our newborn child. It's a baby monitor.

20.

- I can't seem to find the bridle path anywhere

- Horse trail here?

- I hope it's not that far away!

21.

When my pet gerbil died I took him to a taxidermist and she quoted me five grand. I said, "Yeah? You can stuff that then."

22.

My farmer friend once got so drunk he fell head first into a pile of manure. I've never seen him so shitfaced.

23.

My farmer friend didn't take steps against his sheep being rustled yet complained as soon as a couple went missing. I said, "Just let that be a lessen two ewe."

24.

The farmer's sheep are being fleeced. It's shear madness.

25.

[Being interviewed for Farmer's Market licence]

- Full Name?

- Richard Pulsford COS

- What does the 'COS' stand for?

- Nothing. I've just always fancied having lettuce after my name.

26.

Wasps are always sipping other people's drinks. They're so stingy.

27.

I've no idea how the family all caught lice. We've been left scratching our heads.

28.

I had a bad reaction to a bee sting whilst on holiday so went straight to the Tourist Inflammation Service

29.

What's the difference between an indoor arachnid and a burkha? One's a house spider and the other one's a spouse hider.

30.

The man at the zoo with the tranquilizer darts is known as 666 - because he's the number of the beast

31.

Many of Edinburgh zoo's animals are scared of cars, the worst being the feart panda

32.

I was unimpressed by the zoo's 'lion enclosure'. The animals peering out were mere cats.

ART & COMICS

Art

33.

Rubens' portrait 'Girl with a Hacking Cough' really is a phlegmish masterpiece

34.

I was impressed by a sketch of some cutlery at the Van Gogh Museum, one of a top drawer collection

35.

I regretted paying a random street artist do my portrait after realising too late I'd been strangely drawn in

36.

- I once found a Norwegian artist's trousers in a large farm building

- Barn Munch hosen?

- I know it sounds an unlikely story, but I'm no fantasist!

37.

The artist Edward Hopper only had one leg

Comics

38.

Superman - most capeable superhero

39.

Someone just threw a comic at ex-President Trump. I think it was a Walt Disney one. Well whomever it was made Donald duck.

40.

To be beaten by Asterix at boules was particularly Gauling

BAD DAYS

Arguments

41.

Just been threatened by a Frenchman with a bottle of very dry sparkling wine. How very brutish.

42.

I got into an argument with someone on Facebook. She accused me of being flat-chested and looking like a koi carp. I can't remember all the details - I've the mammary of a goldfish.

43.

My ex and I fought over who should get the chocolate sponge pudding. In the end, we both got custardy.

44.

What bugs me, is Russian spies

45.

My German girlfriend is so touchy, especially if I ask her:
"You OK, hun?"

46.

My family don't like it when I casually toss relatives in the
air, but sometimes I'm just in a flip aunt mood

47.

Mrs Schindler: What's wrong, Oskar? You seem listless.

Mr Schindler: (smiling knowlingly) Not at all my dear...
Have you seen my pen anywhere?

48.

My boss thinks I get too frustrated at my inability to
coordinate all the small planes in their shed so he's sent
me on a hangar management course

49.

My accountant said that only when I'd got really angry
with him for losing me money did my assets go up in value
- because you don't appreciate what you've got until
you've lost it

50.

I've been feeling really down because I can't get into
character for the Winnie-the-Pooh musical I'm in but then
everyone says just be Eeyore self

51.

I could have got away with cheating my way to my Duke of Edinburgh's Gold award if it wasn't for those other medalling kids

52.

I've spent all day unsuccessfully trying to fit a catalytic converter and now I'm exhausted

53.

- I'm disappointed with my meteorology exam result. What a miserable morning!

- You've got another grey day?

- No, this time I only got a Grade 'C'

Fights

54.

Don't let on but there's an elephant in the Fight Club
dressing room

55.

I can never let my Spanish friend meet my Dad's sister.
They both fight bulls and it would be the end of the world
if matador met auntie matador.

56.

I once threw a jug in Simon Cowell's face. His face was a
pitcher.

57.

My friend Diane was fatally wounded fighting in the Stirling Castle gift shop. All I had said was, "Di, buy the sword".

58.

I'm obsessed by unusual objects. I find them curios.

59.

My Home Economics teacher was so obsessed with icing, by the end of every lesson I was completely glazed over

60.

My wife said, "I'm sick of your obsession with athletics field events, I'm leaving you." I said, "That's a hammer blow. Come on, give me another shot. Can we at least discus this?"

61.

My wife is obsessed with doing origami. I've told her to try and cut it out.

Problems

62.

My kettle seems to take forever to boil but maybe it's just
one small element of the problem

63.

My problem is I'm such a people-pleaser, and if you don't
like it you can fuck off

64.

This problem with my tadpole seems to be getting worse. It's now growing arms and legs.

65.

I got a brand new helicopter delivered but there's been a problem with starting up the blades. Still, first whirled problems.

BELIEFS

Conspiracies

66.

With the leaking of a highly classified government document we now know that autopsies have been carried out on alien wookies at a second USAF facility in Nevada, known as the Hairier 51

67.

I just found my kids hiding in bed. They said they were afraid to get up after reading all sorts of conspiracy theories. Well I've spoken my mind and made sure they've been thoroughly debunked.

My friend keeps saying 'because I'm so intelligent' I'll come to believe, like him, that the earth is not round, but I'm not falling for such unbelievable flattery

69.

Be warned that scary Greek mythological giants have been seen in the area. The Cyclops is the one I'd wonder most about.

70.

The town council gave me an award for getting all the local sprites to agree not to wreak any more havoc. I'm just glad I could make an imp pact.

71.

When I told my careers adviser I wanted to be a vampire he told me to take a long hard look in the mirror

72.

The giant got angry when he found out how much it would cost for a replacement finger, so boomed in a loud voice: "Fee High, Faux Thumb"

73.

I have a feeling our water source has a creature in it, which somehow gives me a sense of well being

74.

I've written a skit about Boris Johnson which depicts him as a drunken woodland god with a horse's ears and tail. It's a satyrical piece.

75.

- I'm travelling all the way into central London for a talk on one French-born Dutch philosopher

- All Descartes?

- Yeah it's cheaper than buying individual tickets

76.

I went to the local Philosopher's Society. What was I thinking? Still, £3 for a full Plato food - Kant complain.

77.

A thin Pope can't live in Rome but a fatty can

78.

The patron saint of security guards is Saint Francis of a cctv

79.

An excommunicated monk is so out of order

80.

The church is getting delivery of a new font so I'm keeping an eye out for the Courier

81.

- My god has no nose

- How does he smell?

- God nose

82.

- Successful crucifixion?

- Yeah, nailed it!

83.

I've been cleaning the church and using mouthwash. I've found it's most effective with gargoyles.

84.

If I graduated as a Muslim cleric I would celebrate by getting completely mullered

85.

No-one knows how heavy Jesus was when he was born even though there was a weigh-in in a manger

86.

Once you've seen a bishopric you can't unsee it

87.

- I've finally managed to escape from the religious sect which worships padded envelopes

- Jiffy cult?

- They made it really hard for me leave, yes

88.

Jesus got really angry that The Last Supper took place in a confusing set of interconnecting buildings. But then he did have a mass ire complex.

BIRDS

89.

How come geese lay all the eggs, yet get paid less than their male counterparts? Let's finally close the unfair gander pay gap.

90.

I won't click on the link to 'watch this amazing talking hen' as I know it'll just be cluckbait

91.

True fact: Chris Waddle is always followed around by at least 3 penguins

92.

I have been criticised for the way I perform minor surgery on birds but to me it's just like a wart off a duck's back

93.

When I saw there was a pelican crossing outside the church I realised it was a practising Catholic

94.

There are two weird features of the national bird of the African country closest to Madagascar which is nose and beak

95.

When I was able to see a rare bird close up with my telescope it brought a wheatear to my eye

96.

Geneticists have crossed a chicken with a human. Try explaining that to the lay-person.

97.

I ordered a goose online, but was sent a pelican. I knew something was up when I saw the size of the bill.

98.

Two pairs of small birds in my garden must be ill. I know this from the four wrens sick evidence.

THE BODY

Body

99.

I find both women's and men's backsides sexy, but then I'm probably biassed

100.

To prevent chafing while racing a dromedary in the 1500m, use camel mile lotion

101.

I had an osteopath when I was 5, saw a spine specialist when I was 8, and had surgery on two vertebrae as a teenager... but that's enough of my back story...

102.

You know what creases me up, is always forgetting to put some skin conditioner on

103.

Unsure what to call the different parts of your leg? Well call your knee Neil and your heel Helen. Then Bob's your ankle.

104.

Of all the cool reflex checks the simple hammer tap on the leg is the knee test

105.

When I got a facelift, that raised some eyebrows

106.

Having diarrhoea was rather traumatic but I've now found some form of closure

107.

I've just had a health check and apart from my deafness getting worse I was relieved to hear the only other thing I have is some gentle warts

108.

Some people willingly get hours of root canal treatment done. Why? What goes on in these people's heads?

109.

My neighbour is well-endowed, never ill and from Budapest. Oh, and he's a Nazi. He's a well-hung well Hungarian Aryan.

110.

My son asked me what a eunuch was and I said I would not go into detail just willy nilly

111.

I didn't expect to trip while raking the grass and get the implement stuck up me, butt hay hoe

112.

I can't work at the market today as I have a bad sore throat. No point trying to flog while dead hoarse.

113.

My girlfriend says she sympathises for giving me cold sores
but it feels like pain lip surface

114.

I'm sharing nothing with my girlfriend. These are my
carrots and that's herpes.

115.

I refused to pay my optometrist for the reading glasses I was prescribed so I've received a series of letters and the bottom line is I can't make out if anything can be resolved or not

116.

I went to a talk on how much shorter matchsticks are nowadays. I could hardly keep my eyes open.

117.

I thought it was suspicious when I was put in a darkened room then asked if I could make out my will. I mean, that's a pretty unusual eyesight test, right?

118.

Listen to my hard luck story of how I get into fights, causing detached retinas. I might bring a tear to your own eye.

119.

Carrots can help you see in the dark. Just cover them in oil.
Then, set fire to them.

120.

- I don't know what I can use these sheep shears for, the ones I inherited from my friend in West London

- Shepherd's Bush?

- I think he'll want to do his own personal grooming

121.

My little girl was crying because her hair kept going in her face. I told her she had to get a grip.

122.

- I need to try out my new curling tongs on someone and my Mum's sister has volunteered

- Perm an aunt?

- No, the curls won't last forever

123.

My favourite Shakespeare play is the one about comb-overs: Much hairdo about nothing

Sleep

124.

I keep having the same recurring bad dream. It's a
nightmare.

125.

I'm embarrassed taking my gran out for lunch every day as
she's always falling asleep, yet she insists on having her
daily Nan doze.

126.

I couldn't believe it when my TED talk was interrupted - by
my own daughter - who asked me why I was talking to a
stuffed bear and could she get some sleep now

127.

I can't help sleeping with people I've only just met, but
don't judge me - I'm trying my best not to fall asleep at the
Narcolepsy Support Group

128.

I've just tried sleeping on a bed of nails and, I have to say,
I'm very impressed

BOOKS & MAGAZINES

Books

129.

I don't expect E.L. James to be penning a sequel to Lord of the Rings. She's not at all keen.

130.

I dropped my book in the bath earlier. Right now I'm in bed with it, all curled up.

131.

- My new book is set in Persia

- Made it Iranian?

- No, Caspian

132.

The latest Guide to Yorkshire is only available as an e-book

133.

I wasn't excited reading about the type of train leaving Platform 9 and 3/4 from King's Cross as it was mere Rowling stock

134.

I subscribe to 'Fender Monthly'. Every month is a bumper edition.

135.

[At Newsagents]

- What can I get you?

- [continues browsing]

- Hello?

- I'll choose my own magazine, thanks.

- OK!

- [finally making eye contact] I don't like chat

- Well that's narrowed it down slightly

136.

I was waiting to cross the road, along with a chicken. So I joked at the reference, and it laughed so hard, it laid an egg. Well, it's not every day I get a standing ovulation.

137.

Tim Vine's coffin will have the lid velcroed on. What a RIP off!

138.

Stan used to hate it when Ollie wanted to rest on his Laurel

139.

I haven't yet written a good innuendo joke but I'm determined to stick it out

140.

I thought I had a good bird joke but someone said it was shit so I thought yeah, what do guano?

141.

Jimmy Carr is quizmaster in loads of shows. He's such a poser.

142.

I have a joke about badly insulated pubs, inn drafts

COUNTRIES

Countries

143.

Paddington said he left Peru because his mother was too small. As an excuse it really was the bear mini mum.

144.

When my Canadian friend found out her Prime Minister, a one-time martial arts enthusiast, had in the past blacked up, she had mixed feelings about demonstrating trust in judo

145.

The Chinese authorities are battling with a gorilla who keeps ringing people's doorbells. It's a right Hong Kong, King Kong, Ding Dong.

146.

Fun fact: many Cubans are actually round

147.

The Chinese don't like anyone looking into the history of Beijing - so no peeking

148.

I can't remember anything from last year's Luxor to Aswan cruise. I must be getting see Nile dementia.

149.

The G20 leaders are having a meeting. I couldn't tell you who they all are but the Canadian leader is just in.

150.

I would take a bullet for my boss, if we ever have any work meetings in Japan

151.

Russia is having a closing down sale. Everything Moscow!

152.

My UK-based trouser-making business wasn't going well but since moving to Australia I've been making great strides

153.

This guy was telling me how the Swedish car manufacturer he used to work for went bust but I said I wasn't interested in his Saab story

154.

One of the Baltic states has loads of pebbled beaches but I can't remember which one is stonier

155.

The Europeans who take the longest to get the dust out of their carpets are the Slovaks

156.

My hypnotist wants to charge me £500 just for telling me I was Swedish in a past life. He must think I was Bjorn yesterday.

157.

If Barcelona get their region to break away from Spain they might feel Catalonelier

158.

When I feel I have nothing left to live for I remember there's a French guy who owes me dried grapes. He's my raisin debtor.

159.

Not many people know about the French canary who brokered the international peace agreement at the end of World War 1 - the Tweety of Versailles

160.

Of course I can count to five in German. No fear.

CRIME

161.

MI5 have foiled a plot designed to assassinate Prince Charles in Westminster Abbey using a service to heir missile

162.

The village has had its meeting place stolen. The burglars got away with a huge hall.

163.

Whomever it was who stole my classical record collection - they're gonna get a good Haydn

I was once caught stealing a hot air balloon but they let me
go

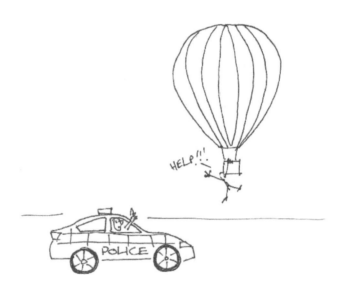

165.

The most pleasant way to be killed is by summery
execution

166.

A man at the donkey sanctuary was killed when one of the
animals sat on him. He was ass-ass-inated.

167.

My uncle was murdered while playing croquet. The jury
said it was manslaughter, but I knew there was mallets
aforethought.

168.

Imagining the total number of killers in the loft is giving me
a psycho sum attic headache

Police

169.

Even if the person riding the prancing horse is a middle-ranking policeman wearing women's clothing, I'm not watching 'dress sarge'

170.

The police tried a gun amnesty in our street, but the kids just gave them daggers

171.

I sustained minor injuries when I was thrown into the police station overnight but the next day I was offered a box of chocolates so I accepted the cell abrasions

172.

The Jersey traffic police just told me to pullover

173.

The Met are swarming all over London giving out gold handcuffs for Christmas, in what has been described as heavy police presents

174.

- The police stopped me for being drunk on a stag do,
covered in foam cream

- Pissed, all whipped?

- No, just a fixed penalty fine

175.

I punched my neighbour after he forced me to grit his
driveway and jump start his car, and now I'm the one
being arrested for a salt and battery

176.

A number of MPs are set to make a speech today on
policing. I reckon we'll see seven orate.

DEATH

Death

177.

Apparently Jonathon Ross wants everyone to toast him with Scotch at his funeral. I think that's a rather whisky undertaking.

178.

In Devon, a dead cow is called an Exmooer

179.

I work in a mortuary. It's dead cool.

180.

I'm never going to inherit much, even with the best will in the world

181.

Pavarotti's funeral arrangements were no small bier

182.

I won my local séance competition hands down

183.

The best person to get the pips out of an apple is Derek a'Corer

184.

My brother once paid loads of money to train as a medium. I don't know what possessed him.

DRIVING

185.

I just saw a sports car, driven by a scantily-clad young sheep. It was in a lamb bikini.

186.

Why aren't self-driving cars called autoautomobiles?

187.

This morning I seized the chance to instant message the garage and buy the Fiat I'd reserved. I simply had to car-pay DM.

188.

Seems I've been sold a car with a faulty exhaust so I am fuming

189.

The man from the AA said I'd never be able to stop the car with those worn out disk pads. I said, "Give me a brake."

190.

The tat at my car boot sale may be disorganised but then you can buy almost anything except the kitsch in sync

191.

When my back was turned in the garden my son dropped his old model Japanese car into my G&T. So when he said, "Datsun in your ice!" I said, "Yeah, I'll have to put some sunglasses on."

192.

I asked the local garage if they could arrange a bigger car for me but somehow they just made my current one vanish

193.

All of the queen's attendants have to use curtsey cars

ENVIRONMENT

The Council

194.

The council needs to save money and all our park keeper does is count the flowers growing out of the grass. Surely his daisies are numbered.

195.

- I've seen transvestites are working for the council

- Bin men?

- I think they still are. They're just wearing women's clothing.

196.

Our local council are so keen to make the buses run on time, they're pulling out all the stops

197.

Wind turbine impressions? Well I'm a massive fan.

198.

Some rebels at The Forestry Commission have formed their own splinter group

199.

I'm still waiting for the Green Party to install a window in my festival tent - they promised they would camp pane for me

200.

It's unlikely you're going to care much about retaining EU environmental protections if your name is Jacob Re-Smog

201.

As the arctic warms up we must make decisions on what to do about the polar bears now. These things can't just be defurred.

Rubbish

202.

Guess what the council have given me to put my household waste in? Only a rubbish bin.

203.

What's the difference between the illegal dumping of waste and Oliver Hardy? One is fly tipping and the other one is tie flipping.

204.

I was the sole organiser behind the march against fly tipping. Litter rally.

205.

I was sick of the ex-wife's clutter so I told her I was getting rid of all her junk. And that's where our relationship ended, just as we reached the council dump. Well that was the tipping point.

EXERCISE

Cycling

206.

Popeye didn't mind getting chafing from cycling. He said you can never have too much spin itch.

207.

Who is the bicycle wheel manufacturer's spokes person?

Fitness

208.

I'm on a drug which keeps me healthy. I'm fit, I mean.

209.

I was at the gym when my calf went. I got home later to find someone had left the farm gate open.

210.

I'm raising money for charity by selling my stomach muscles at bargain prices, as I lower myself from the gym's roof on a rope. It's a sponsored abs sale.

211.

I've given up on personal fitness consultants - my bum actually looks bigger in running gear now, thanks to my added ass trainers

212.

I watched a bodybuilder on the beach string lots of shells together with copper wire. He must have been flexing his mussels.

FLYING

213.

Do bi-planes ever want to go straight?

214.

Our childminder is organising a sponsored aeroplane jump to raise funds for the village's New Year's do. Yes it's 'Parachute a Nanny' for the Parish Hootenanny.

215.

- After my flight from the Middle East I developed a hacking cough

- Qatar airways?

- Yeah, it's hard to breathe with all that phlegm

216.

The most popular menu choice in the UK Border Force canteen is Seize a Salad

217.

My Dad's so proud of me - he thinks I'm in charge of directing aircraft into and out of Prestwick airport, when really I work on the roads putting out the cones, at Ayr traffic control

218.

Only one skydiving company was fined last year for breaching safety standards. But regulators said that was just a drop in the ocean.

219.

I wanted to explain all my planned aerial shots of the airport but security just wouldn't let me drone on about it

220.

As my wife tried flying my new drone I let slip how expensive it was and she nearly hit the roof

FOOD

Food

221.

If you're unsure which dairy products are best for your health just go with yogurt instinct

222.

I told the doctor I have no energy. He said I should rest and give up milk products so I've cleared my dairy for the weak.

223.

I said to the wife, "What's that you're cooking with?"

She said, "It's spelt flour"

I said, "Never mind how it's spelt, what is it?"

224.

I always cook pasta at a moderately slow tempo as apparently it's best when it's done andante

225.

Not done this before but thought I'd try making some asparagus soup. Anyone got any good tips?

226.

I've been cheesemaking. Whey to go!

227.

I've just eaten a whole load of asparagus soaked in alcohol and I'm feeling rather tips-y

228.

I can make a meat and cheese sandwich using both hands. I'm ham brie dexterous.

229.

Times are hard so I've been cooking with pigs' snouts and tails just to make ends meat

230.

The soup I made gave me mild constipation. I had a mini strainey.

231.

I just sent a food parcel to my first wife. Fed Ex.

232.

My local deli will only ever make ricotta cheese. I've said to them, "Why does it always have to be that whey?"

233.

I'm sick of my girlfriend eating eggs all the time. It's ova between us.

234.

[Royal Family dinner party on Zoom]

- [Charles] Is everyone enjoying their grilled quail?

- [All, except The Queen] Yes!

- [Camilla] Liz, are you on mute?

- [The Queen] Yes - one is queen, so one is enjoying swan

235.

I'm taking a kebab into the library for lunch today as they're always telling me to shish it

236.

I'd give blood if they offered a donor kebab afterwards

237.

I always carry my donor card with me - because you never know when you might be in need of a kebab

238.

The biggest takeaway from the G7 summit was on the last night when Joe Biden ordered a huge kebab and couldn't finish it

239.

I said to the French waiter, "Bring me the Eiffel tower on a plate" and he said, "That's a tall order, sir"

240.

- I walked 20 miles so I could eat at a fancy restaurant, but got blisters on my feet

- Suppurating?

- I'd give them 4 stars

241.

When I asked the waiter for the menu he pointed out the gas and water pipes. So I said, "Is that all you've got for mains?"

242.

Due to misunderstandings at the Jamaican buffet restaurant, I had to modify what I said to the customers, from "You have to go for the jerk yourself, off at the counter over there", to "Can you do that in the privacy of the toilets please"

FRUIT & VEG & PLANTS

Allotments

243.

I'm writing a book about the local allotment holders who suddenly get rich when someone buys their fruit to use in the world's biggest cocktail. It's full of amazing plot twists.

244.

When I read the council letter which said my allotment had more weeds than vegetables, well, I lost the plot

245.

I bumped into one of the older men from the allotment association and he said he'd been buying vegetables and viagra. He said it wasn't realistic to expect him to spend all his spare time trying to grow his own.

Fruit

246.

I didn't feel bad for swearing at the WI lady in jam making class after she told me to stop eating the fruit. She said I only jarred a bit.

247.

My habit of stealing from greengrocers was inspired by Nick Berry

248.

I once found myself sat between Courteney Cox and Russell Crowe. It was a potential banana skin, as a gooseberry on a date between an apple and a kiwi.

249.

People ask me why I only eat dried fruit but all I'll say is, I have my raisins

250.

- Hello, I would like to return this appliance as it's not extracting the juice from fruit and vegetables as advertised. I have the receipt.

- D'you, sir?

- Yes, that's what it's called

251.

My girlfriend wants me to eat more tropical fruit but I'd really guava not

252.

Someone has clipped my hedges into the shapes C, B and A. It's topiary out of order.

253.

The seed I planted just said "Acht" as it sprouted out of the soil. Nice to see it German eight.

254.

I'm a sucker for propagating plants

255.

Pink Floyd and Led Zeppelin will be represented on Gardeners' World today as Roger Waters Robert Plant

256.

My friend told me, "I forgot to water my house plants. Do you think I've killed them?" I said, "Why don't you just give them some water and see what transpires."

257.

The writer of The Madness of George III has put fruit on his head. Gourd on Bennett.

258.

I hear my friend's got a vegetable patch, so maybe he's finally decided to quit smoking his greens

259.

Unlike the other tourists outside Buckingham Palace I wasn't going to stand and watch a choreographed delivery of fresh greengroceries. I'm not bothered about the changing of the gourd.

GOOD DAYS

Good Moods

260.

I've finally found someone to assist me with my escapology act. Well I can hardly contain myself.

261.

I'm feeling all emotional as I've been selected to make apple crumble for the queen. I just hope I can keep it together.

262.

I felt very proud when I showed my stamp collection to a philatelist and he said all my stamps were first class

263.

I just broke my personal best for keepy-uppy. Although it may be cheating as I'm on Viagra.

264.

The last job I was offered was with a sun cream manufacturer. They said they were impressed with the way I had applied myself.

265.

I received my knighthood from Cilla Black when I won a competition on her programme. The first I knew of it, was when she picked me out of the audience and said: "Surprise sir prize!"

Fairs

266.

I've been fined unreasonably for trying to test drive the dodgems. Why can't I have a fair trial?

267.

The man in charge of the dodgems demanded payment so I gave it to him balanced on my stuck up middle finger. It was a token gesture.

Holidays

268.

I went on the trans-Siberian railway and arrived in
Vladivostock as a woman

269.

I needed advice on whether I could keep my hands on my
arms while on holiday, so I rang the two wrist information
office - who then gave me the finger

270.

My holiday was a let down. The rep said he'd take me
whale watching. But we ended up in Jerusalem, just
looking at this big wall.

271.

I went on holiday to Sicily and found the place was
mobbed

272.

I've just discovered two deep holes in my garden with water in them. Well well.

273.

Maybe a dozen local parks have lost much of their grass in the recent dry spell, though that's just a bald park figure

274.

I had just put new gloves on for rock climbing in unusually adverse weather conditions when I lost my grip and fell, but it seems trite to just blame it all on climb mitt change

275.

I was surprised to see a line of North Africans out in the snow today eating grilled food as it wasn't exactly Berber queue weather

276.

I've just been listening to the shipping forecast. Doesn't sound like there'll be much shipping.

HOUSES

Builders

277.

Why do builders always use quick-setting concrete? It's not like there's a harden fast rule.

278.

Our builders were a bunch of cowboys. They threatened to shoot me when I said I would Sioux.

279.

Bob the Builder had plans to retire to an island in the Mediterranean but that was before we left the EU. Can he fix it? By adopting local citizenship, Corsican.

280.

- My child fell in the cement mixer yesterday evening

- Sunset?

- Yeah, he's stuck fast in there

281.

And now the results of the voting in this year's most dilapidated buildings awards. In the Country and City categories... it's all gone to Iraq and Rouen.

282.

My attempts at stopping our house subsiding were nothing to right home about

283.

We were worried we couldn't afford our electricity bill, but instead of disconnecting us nPower offered us a simple solution, and now we're de-lighted

284.

Maybe the way to stop aliens getting into my house is by reinforcing the roof. Or maybe resistance is few tile.

285.

Feng Shui advice is you have all your kitchen cabinets facing northwards. We're fine, as ours were fitted by Magnet.

286.

The electric trip switch just went but I'm re-fusing to fix it

287.

Doorbells. You can't knock 'em.

288.

Someone thought it would be funny to leave a drawing pin on my chair. What a bloody cheek!

289.

Many older houses stay well-preserved, looking smooth and shiny - the ones that use a good fab brick conditioner

290.

Is the collective noun for rolls of patterned wallpaper, a flock?

291.

The sofa and chairs in my wigwam form a nice teepee's suite

292.

- Help! My bath is leaking round the edges. What will fix it, and where can I get it?

- New sealant?

- Is there nowhere closer?

293.

- This light bulb says '60' on it

- That's wattage

- I'd say it's at least five years old

ILLNESS

Covid

294.

Channel 4 should make a programme where loving couples compete for the worst Covid symptoms: The Great British Bae Cough

295.

In one Sage meeting Chris Witty illustrated a chart with the Greek God of War and Guy Garvey but Matt Hancock had to ask which was which as he didn't know his Ares from his Elbow

296.

- To prepare myself for the jab I had a fag (and disposed of it) then meditated in just my underwear

- Ashtray Zen knickers?

- No, Pfizer's

297.

Have you noticed how everyone getting their Covid jab looks younger these days

298.

The local rabbits are not socially distancing. The police have issued arrest warrens.

299.

If I get vaccinated against car owner virus will I become auto immune?

300.

My mum used to say the way to a man's heart is through his stomach, which is why she never passed her cardiothoracic surgery exams

301.

The patient next to me in A&E - who had a pen stuck up her nose - asked me what I was in for. I said, "Don't be such a Nosey Parker".

302.

There's a really attractive doctor who works in the spinal injuries unit. I bet she's turned a few heads.

303.

I find hospital parking really difficult. I can never find a parking space big enough for a hospital.

304.

Well, well, well, well, well, well, well, well, well! Looks like there's a hospital in Dundee.

305.

NHS24 said I should go straight to the hospital with the rash I described, so I stuffed some pyjamas into my daughter's Minnie Mouse gym bag and ran. At the hospital, they said it was the worst case they'd ever seen.

306.

I had thought of getting a wrist operation done at my local plastic surgeon's but I'm having second thoughts as they've recently changed hands

Children

307.

At my age it's going to be difficult to get down with the kids, and even harder to get up again

308.

I helped my son get accepted into the British Puppet Guild. It was all legit - I just had to pull a few strings.

309.

Someone has just accused me of wanting to kidnap their children. Well I would take issue with that.

310.

Teenagers tattooing themselves - what do youth ink?

311.

- My Dad's home brew used to make us all ill

- What was wrong with it?

- Well, it wasn't actually clear

312.

My friend is giving laxatives to his elderly dad - in case he's
had too much Imodium and he clogs his pop

313.

I always like to surprise my Dad on Father's Day with a big
'ta-da'

314.

I told my nephews they could eat as many crisps as they
wanted before dinner and they looked sceptical but I said,
"You may scoff..."

315.

My granddad says that when he goes he wants to be
surrounded by his family but it's hard for us all to fit into
his bathroom

316.

My mother was a poor swimmer and always wanted me to
hold her in the pool - which is why I was called a Mummy's
buoy

317.

- My Scottish 6-year-old nephew keeps pooing in his new class

- P2?

- No, just poo

318.

- My niece is in her final year at school in Chelmsford

- S6?

- Yes, in that county

319.

When the teacher told me I wasn't going to be added to the top maths class I was non-plussed

Studying

320.

I tried a damp proof course but now wish I'd studied something more interesting

321.

A specific part of the brain of large African river animals makes them clever enough to go to their own university, which is the hippo campus

322.

I feel like I'm always in the firing line. I'm never first in the queue for the kiln at pottery class.

323.

My son is lodging with some archaeology students and he says their digs are awful

324.

It took me 6 hours to learn basic semaphore. After that I was flagging.

325.

- I'm applying to go on that aromatherapy course but I can't keep using the word 'smell' in the application

- Fragrant?

- Yeah, I'll need to get funding from somewhere

326.

My brother told me he'd been on a navigation course. I asked him, "How did you find it?"

MUSIC

Musical Instruments

327.

My girlfriend gave her reasons as to why it was OK to play
a stringed instrument while we chatted but to me it
sounded terribly convo luted

328.

A drummer's comfort level is measured per cushion

329.

- I can play pop songs on any instrument you like

- How about a bassoon?

- Sure. Give me a minute and I'll play Waterloo.

330.

Everyone should swallow a brass instrument whole like I
did - and I'm not going to apologise for my pro tuba rants

331.

- I've been adding some extra padding to the piano seats

- Soft stools?

- Yeah. I must stop eating those fig rolls.

332.

I wanted to learn the trumpet so now I have my own tooter

333.

What type of instrument can you poke Highland cattle with? Anything as long as it's a coo stick.

334.

I read about someone in Prague who is solely responsible for making sure statues of Dvořák are level. I thought, who still rights Czechs?

335.

- I've been reading about this jazz pianist who lived in terrible conditions

- Flat squalor?

- Yeah, that's him!

336.

I really enjoyed going to the opera. It had a Carmen effect on me.

OCCASIONS

Dancing

337.

When I flew into Heathrow I had to show my passport and take part in some Morris dancing. Apparently everyone now has to go through customs.

338.

It's Friday tomorrow so I'm going to wear lots of lycra. My colleagues will be oblivious as I'll be twerking from home.

339.

I'm useless at twerking in Spanish. I can't roll my arse.

340.

I was watching the big dance scene in a period drama on TV when I was distracted by the FA Cup game on my phone. It's not the first time I've been court ball watching.

341.

- I was born on the cusp of Cancer and Leo

- July baby?

- It's the truth, honey!

342.

The barman said that as it was his birthday I could have
two bottles of tequila for free. I took it all with more than
a pinch of salt.

343.

I'm having mildly spiced chicken to mark my birthday so
there's some sense of a Cajun

344.

My wife said she was buying me a radio for my birthday,
one which didn't need electricity or batteries. I thought,
that's got to be a wind up.

345.

I can officiate for you at book launches, ship launches, baptisms, christenings... you name it...

346.

- I've invented a decorated cardboard tube which explodes when two people pull on its ends to release party hats and small trinkets

- But that's a cracker

- Why, thank you!

347.

Me: Are you going to attend my inheritance allocation
decisions party?

Her: Will do

Me: Thanks - I was looking for a more succinct name for it

348.

I need to look for a medieval-themed party costume, so
I'm off to serf the web

349.

When I worked at Heinz I offered to organise the annual
office party. They loved my can do attitude.

350.

A witch cast the same spell on me at two different parties,
giving me the strangest deja voo do feeling

351.

I'm off to a bishop's fancy dress party. I'm Right Revved up for it.

352.

I've started making my fifth pair of shoes for a Harry Potter '70s themed party but it seems appropriate to stop at platform 9 and three quarters

ON STAGE

Magic

353.

For my magic trick I will conjure up a dead body wearing a brassiere, using the magic words "A bra cadaver"

354.

- Why have you written ancient-looking magical lettering on that red stone?

- It's my rune

- OK, it's maroon, but what kind of magic are you doing?

355.

The magician said think of a number so I imagined being out on a really cold day without gloves on

356.

It's panto season again, so here's a shout out to those
three animals who always make a sneaky appearance: "It's
bee, hind, ewe!"

357.

I used to do silent impressions of a vase of mine but few
people appreciate my Ming

358.

To earn some cash I've been reduced to performing mime.
There are no words.

359.

My musical on ice has received nothing but chorus skating
reviews

360.

Our play about the German army in WW1 has had to be cancelled, due to Hun force scene circumstances

361.

Someone has to take everything down after the theatre production ends. It's de rigeur.

362.

The sisters in Macbeth all had cystitis according to the play witch wee sore

PETS

Cats

363.

I've just broken up with Catwoman over the way she speaks. I said, "It's me, not mew."

364.

My cat's been marking its territory. It gave it a no.1 out of 10, which was a wee bit on the low side.

365.

A good first pet would be a young cat. See it as a kind of starter kit.

366.

If my cat knew I plan to incorporate him into the brick wall
when he dies he'd be mortarfied

367.

- My cat has some strange ways of grooming herself

- Foibles?

- Yeah, she gets them frequently

368.

I'm not lying - my dog retrieved a stick from half a mile away, far-fetched as it sounds

369.

My dog's always running off, but today I found him in the auction house, and for once was pleased with what he fetched (which was a lot)

370.

Never done this before but I'm thinking of setting up some kennels. Can anyone give me a few pointers?

371.

We've discovered our trainee guide dog is lactose intolerant so he's never going to mutt the custard

372.

My dog's gone into the farmer's field. It's a worry.

373.

My friend said "My pet duck's feathers keep ruffling" so I explained what to do about it. She looked confused, so I said, "Do you want me to right that down for you?"

374.

For sage advice I turn to Skippy. My pet can guru.

375.

I botched a repair job on my rabbit's home, thus invalidating the warren

376.

Pets are a backward step

377.

Our first trial pet was a guinea pig

378.

The recent cutbacks to paddocks are largely down to government horse territory measures

379.

The government wants to micromanage everything down to the smallest level, like a nano state

380.

Brexit is affecting the importing of Mediterranean fruit such as figs and prunes, but it's too early to say whether it'll also bring an end to freedom of movement

381.

Nigel Farage's favourite South Central Asian country is Alfgarnettstan

382.

The sweetest PM was Sherbert Asquith

383.

When I tried to gift Nigel Farage a bonsai he said he wouldn't accept anything foreign. I should have known he'd be happier with some bigger tree.

384.

- A cannibal broke into no.10. yesterday evening and had Boris Johnson for dinner

- Ate PM?!

- I don't know what time it happened

385.

- Boris Johnson has said he's decided to cut out the lies and be totally honest with everyone, from tomorrow

- De-fib, real later?!!!

- Yeah, keep one handy. Some people might have a heart attack when they hear this news.

386.

The Brexit Secretary wants to kick off every meeting with 'God Save the Queen'. Personally, I wouldn't stand for it.

RELATIONSHIPS

Dating

387.

Even though the speed dating event for Sean Connery fans had to share the room with the chicken pox relapse support group, everyone enjoyed their 'shingles night'

388.

I've found out my new girlfriend lives in the next block of flats and I'm just about to call on her for the first time. I'm buzzing.

389.

Tinder isn't exactly setting things on fire for me - for one thing, I can never find any matches

390.

My girlfriend is a stunner. She works in an abattoir.

Flirting

391.

I met an attractive lady at the French embassy who said she was a charge d'affaires. I said I was very interested in a liaison but I would need to get some Euros first.

392.

The hotel waitress asked me if I wanted the cooked breakfast and I said I wanted the full complement, and she said, "OK, one cooked breakfast, everything, for a very handsome-looking man."

393.

It's no surprise that the hot-looking flirty woman won the cookery competition instead of me but I have to remind myself it's the baking tart that counts

394.

My fiancé is the one in the rubber top and pencil skirt -
that's my bride 2B

395.

A rumour went round the stag party the groom-to-be was
only drinking water so I soon scotched that one for him

396.

I proposed to my girlfriend at the local duck pond. I got
down on one knee.

397.

I thought about cancelling my wedding when I was given a
ticket to see Mark E Smith instead, but everyone warned
me that the bride comes before The Fall

SCIENCE

Science/Maths

398.

Charles Darwin was judging a naturist competition when he first developed his idea of au naturel selection

399.

When biologists make a new discovery they love to work out if it's feline, ovular or ocular, as they have to cat, egg or eyes everything

400.

A new study is out, and it seems that lions make the loudest noise, going by the roar data

401.

A newspaper once ran a series of articles by Stephen Hawking on underwear through the ages. It was called The Times History of Briefs.

402.

My son is learning his times tables so I asked him what is 4 x 4 and he said it's a two-axled vehicle drivetrain capable of providing torque to all of its wheels simultaneously. So I've parked that one.

403.

One of the Norse gods was so bad at maths class he stuck out like a Thor sum

404.

I walked all the way up to the admin office on the top floor to borrow a calculator. Now I feel unwell so I might take the lift back. I think I may be coming down with sum thing.

405.

I've been trying to work out how many cough sweets I've got but I'm no good at menthol arithmetic

406.

My Darth Vader impression sucks

407.

My packet of herbs is dated May 2031. Does this mean that thyme travel really does exist?

SEX

Porn

408.

You've got to laugh at some porn films. The ones with clowns in them anyway. Nothing comes funnier.

409.

I thought my girlfriend had gone off me but she's been busy streamlining her aircon business and, incredibly, says she's trebled her income with only fans

410.

It's unlikely Trump has slept with any porn stars - they've often had breast implants and he hates Fake Nudes

411.

I just read about some goalkeepers who got a mere ticking off for sending dick pics to some of their club's fans. Surely they need to face stiffer penalties.

412.

Edinburgh zoo's pandas have been mating - after watching bird porn. Well, what's sauce for the goose is sauce for the panda.

413.

It's quite possible to be polyamorous and still like a cockatoo

414.

I'm getting aroused watching this frightened Tibetan ox on a merry-go-round - it's like an afraid dizzy yak

415.

What is it about those sexy dolled-up Cambodian communists, with their 'Come 'ere Rouge' look

416.

Guys, I'll be giving away some viagra next week. Thought you might like the heads up.

417.

I got my sleeping pills mixed up with my viagra. Well that was one big cock up.

418.

My girlfriend said she wanted a 'weird weekend' - a threesome, with a documentary filmmaker. I tell you, I'm so Theroux with her.

419.

I found this naked man in my girlfriend's bedroom. When he saw me, he soon got his come up pants.

420.

The neighbours complained to the police about our noisy lovemaking. The officers who turned up asked me if I would come quietly.

421.

I keep joking to my girlfriend I'm always just reusing the same condom and she says it's really wearing a bit thin

422.

I opened my friend's cupboard by mistake and saw it was full of leather gear. Sometimes you get unexpected gimps into people's private lives.

423.

I just found out my wife's been having an affair with an auctioneer. I said, "How long has this been going, going, on?"

424.

My wife's said she's going to arouse me by trying to draw my favourite cartoon character on her breasts but I think she's just making a Bod for her own rack

425.

Sounds to me as if swingers would enjoy shopping at 'Adult Я Us'

SHOES & WALKING

Shoes

426.

My uncle wears size 15 shoes. Surely no mean feet.

427.

- My laces keep coming undone. I am not pleased.

- Try a double knot

- I am not not pleased

- There you go, you're feeling better already!

428.

My mate John Lewis always gets new shoes before the old ones wear out. He's never knowingly undersoled.

429.

I tried Platform 9 and 3/4 but I could hardly walk in them

430.

[At Balmoral]

[Camilla] What do you think, Charlie - can we go hiking?

[Charles] No, Cams. No-one can address me that way 'til Mummy's dead.

431.

We were lost on a mountain walk and the map made no sense to me but we found our way back after my mate interpreted all the map's symbols correctly. Legend.

432.

I asked a passing hillwalker if he knew the way to the top of the mountain and he pointed downwards. Well I knew summit must be up.

Betting

433.

The Arctic lottery is open to all natives with identical
siblings. You have to be Inuit twin it.

434.

I put a tenner on a horse at Newmarket but it was wasted.
My tenner ended up two miles away at the finishing line.

435.

Why does the European Central Bank only makes Euro coins. It doesn't make cents.

436.

I'd rather keep my money in a leather wallet. You can't purse suede me otherwise.

437.

The cash machine is temporarily out of order so it's no cash atm

438.

Our carpet fitter wanted cash upfront and used sellotape to hold the carpets down, yet denied he was a tacks avoider

439.

Fashion shops are warning of an imminent shortage of items and, by spring, we can expect skirts to be severely depleated

Shops

440.

I've been shopping all morning for army uniforms and now
I'm getting fatigued

441.

When I worked at the sandwich shop I was allowed to take
home the leftover meat. It was a pork of the job.

442.

[Hugh Laurie, in his local shop]

- The card machine's broken. Can you pay by cash, Hugh?

- I would but I have a nut allergy

443.

I tried scanning my book of tree poems at the checkout
but it didn't like the bark ode

444.

I saw a sign nailed to the wall in my local corner shop, which read "No-one has ever successfully shoplifted from this shop. So don't think you'll be any different." I thought, I don't know how to take that.

445.

I took a chair in for repairs. The shop owner said, "I can do it for 50 quid. Plus VAT. Would you like a reseat for that?"

446.

I love working in retail as much as the Next person

447.

I'm told Harrods can't sell chilled food items but can Selfridges?

448.

How difficult can it be for Sainsbury's to label their iceberg lettuce correctly? It's not rocket signs, is it.

SONGS & SINGERS

Bands

449.

The Beach Boys were always generous with getting the beers in. I'd offer to get them, but they'd always insist: "Round, round, get a round, I'll get a round."

450.

- I hate Bono and his band

- What, you too?

451.

Another 28, and boy band E-17 would have been as good as Cream

452.

I was drummer in a support band for Guns n' Roses. No sooner had I met their guitarist and he's asking me for a cymbal. I said, "That's a bit / "

453.

According to this press release Chris Martin is now playing keyboards using only his toes and heels. What a story! I'll need to check the footnotes.

454.

Has Jean Michel Jarre ever actually played the O2?

455.

Today I'll flip my pancakes to three points of the compass, but not to the fourth as I couldn't give a toss for One Direction

456.

I have just acquired a rare Jethro Tull item. This is not a drill.

457.

When I was a security guard at the mall I would get rid of the kids hanging around Santa's grotto at closing time by telling them that 'Elves have left the building!'

458.

I missed Edith Piaf singing at the bird sanctuary, but you know, Jay Egret Wren

459.

Sting loved syncopated rhythms. I can't recall ever seeing the Police on the beat.

460.

I wish I had invested in Botox manufacturers. Cher's are through the roof.

461.

The rudest singers are The Pointer Sisters

462.

My favourite singer likes to make jelly moulds in the shape of fictional Greek islands and native New Zealanders. That's Atlantis Maori set.

463.

In the UK, American singer Johnny Mathis is known as Johnny Mathsis

Songs

464.

Times are hard for singers and actors. I hear it was a cruel summer, and Robert de Niro's waiting.

465.

Oasis have promised to get me round with Pam Nestor, Shane MacGowan and Suzi Quatro to drink liquers and watch the footie and moan about the Video Assistant Referee system. So some day you will find me in with Pam, Shane, Sue, Pernod, VAR on the Sky.

466.

Do you know where they built our house? In the middle of our street! Yeah, it's Madness!

467.

- Why are you weeping?

- I caught my eye on the corner of that Beatles sheet music

- Loose leaf in the eye with dire moans?

- No, 'Let It Be', but the actual song is irrelevant

468.

When Liam Neeson broke down two passing field marshals offered to help. They took his car to the local garage and sang to his kids: "Head soldiers, Neeson tows Neeson tows..."

469.

Julie Andrews asked me, "What language, drink and food shall we learn about this week?" I said, "Diary me Farsi, latte, dough" and she said, "Can we move on from the tonal scales, please!"

470.

Someone once said to me as a child "Where's your mama gone?"

I said, "She's gone off with a Nepalese mountain guide in an off-terrain vehicle"

She said, "Sherpa, sherpa, jeep, jeep?"

I said, "No, there was only one of each."

471.

I hear Neil Diamond has already had 3 of his 5 fruit and veg portions today: Swede, Carrot, Lime...

472.

I was being shoved about from one ward to another, yet the guy doing it just shrugged, saying 'Anything goes'. He really was a cold porter.

473.

Raindrops on roses - flavourless (2/10)

Crisp apple strudels - tasty (8/10)

Schnitzel with noodles - yummy (9/10)

- These are a few of my flavour rate things

474.

Our musical theatre group is currently touring Wales and we didn't finish our production of Mary Poppins until 2am last night because the villagers in Llanfairpwllgwyngyllgogerychwyrndrobwllllantysiliogogog-och requested 3 encores of 'Supercalifragilisticexpialidocious'

475.

I had just had a new bath put in when Lionel Richie comes prancing into the bathroom, and I said, "Lionel! Will you stop dancing on the sealant."

Games

476.

My Geordie friend blames online gaming for his binge cheese eating. He says he gets lost in his own world of wor Kraft.

477.

As we played a role-playing board game my mum fell to the floor and said "I am an emergency response medical vehicle" and I said, "Shall I just call you an ambulance?"

478.

My Mate had to leave his game of human battleships early so asked me to go on as a sub

479.

The bowling alley wants us to play a game with a pin missing but how can that be tenable?

480.

When Spielberg played Hawking at Connect Four it was even-Stevens

481.

My girlfriend is stuck inside a virtual reality game. She's completely inconsoleable.

482.

My kids are playing a science versus religion game. Nothing profound, just astronauts and crosses.

483.

My friend asked me if I would like a game of backgammon. I said, "No - I hate backgammon!" He said, "How about Draughts?" I said, "No. I hate that as well!" He said, "Hate chess too?" I said, "Don't even get me started on that high-speed rail project!"

484.

I've been playing a game with the kids where we're not allowed to step off the furniture because the carpet is full of poisonous caterpillars. It's called 'the floor is larvae'.

485.

In the warm up, I accidentally kicked the rugby ball over the goalposts but could I have done that if I'd actually tried?

486.

Here's a rare shout out to cricket umpires

487.

Found a rather downbeat old diary entry from my first day at cricket training: "Kept behind at wicket-keeping class"

488.

I thought I had kept my crossdressing under wraps while batting for my cricket team until the day I was caught out in the slips

489.

Our lunchtime game of football ended 'ate all'

490.

My sibling always wanted me to go in goal but I would say "Am I my brother's keeper?"

491.

As they want fewer people attending football matches, I think we need to take a stand

492.

The team was short of a defender so they asked me if I knew of anyone who could fill in for them. I thought for a moment then said: "I'll be right back..."

493.

Apparently the romantic hero in Pride and Prejudice was a big Derby County supporter and one-time striker. I'll be honest, I wouldn't have had him down in my fan Darcy football.

494.

- My best friend Mick has left to play for a football team in Germany and he's irreplaceable

- Bye! Yearn new Mick?

- No, Borussia Moenchengladbach

495.

The man who invented the system of racing car flags has had a chequered history

496.

For coverage of the Grand Prix, press the F1 key

497.

There's a 100m race for older men? Balder dash.

498.

Boxing? What's that a bout?

499.

I'm a big fan of the parallel bars. Not so much gymnastics, more easy pub crawls.

SWEETS

Chocolate

500.

Just when I'd overcome my addiction to needing chocolate powder on my coffee, the barista goes and puts the mochas on it

501.

I opened the window, and as the smell of gold-wrapped chocolates wafted in, it was like a breath of Ferrero Rocher

502.

I once went backstage at a Stranglers gig and ate all their chocolates. They then went out and did a heartfelt rendition of "No more Heroes any more."

503.

Someone told me Fletcher Christian loved eating chocolate bars. It's all new to me on the Bounty.

504.

Despite complimenting the taxi driver, she refused to move when I accidentally squashed a chocolate orange on the seat. Flat Terry's got me nowhere.

505.

I'm told it's mandatory for shops in Amsterdam to sell chocolate willies. Why the dick tat?

506.

My son said hum us a tune so I put some mashed
chickpeas on a cough sweet

507.

I always want to eat meringue with cream whenever I hear
the chimes of Big Ben. It must be a pavlovan response.

508.

No-one wanted to come into the café after some toddlers
spread their ice creams over everything. In fact, the whole
place was desserted.

509.

For sale: One packet of polos. Mint condition.

510.

You need to know now what maple syrup is, ASAP!

511.

- The wife scrapes the pan when she's making jam and it hurts my ears

- Jarrs a lot?

- She fills about a dozen at a time

TEA & COFFEE & DRINKS

Coffee

512.

The barista asked me if he should put powder on my cappuccino, and I said "I should cocoa".

513.

I had a look round a coffee magnate's estate. 'Maxwell House' was uninspiring but you should have seen the grounds.

514.

When I demonstrated my new electric teaspoon at the coffee morning it caused quite a stir

515.

I've been having a coffee mourning. My espresso machine died.

Drinks

516.

My girlfriend wants me to lose weight. She tries to entice me with sugar free drinks, but I won't be swayed by her Diet Coax

517.

- I'm struggling to carry this crate of bottled water

- Evian?

- Yeah, it weighs more than the Perrier

518.

I used to do research into alternative sugared beverages but the only thing I actually developed was two types of diet beet teas

519.

My religious friend thinks Jesus turned water into camomile tea. Well that's just herbal leafs.

520.

Why aren't motorway services called Tea Junctions?

521.

The family wonder why I get so worked up about keeping hold of my mug and not wanting to share their germs but I have to point out it's just not everyone's cup of tea

522.

I've spilt a hot drink on my top and now I can't wear this Green Tea shirt

TECHNOLOGY

Phones

523.

I've had an implant in one of my testicles which allows me to take phone calls through it. Really it's no great medical breakthrough, purely SIM bollock (I am of course talking bollocks).

524.

Yes, your honour, it was my client who covered your mobile phone with gold leaf while it was plugged in. Pleading gilty as charged.

525.

My new phone wouldn't power up but the retailer said I could send it back, without charge

526.

Found an old mobile phone from 20 years ago. I upgraded it to a smart phone by making it a little suit and a cable tie.

527.

My sister asked me if I had the power cable for her phone
and I said 'Guilty as charged'

528.

I didn't realise what was showing on the screen behind me
in my zoom call with the NSPCC. They said I should have
first gone through suitable background checks.

Photos / Videos

529.

I've taken photos of my Cornish pasties lunch. I've posted them on Ginstergram.

530.

Developing countries are great for getting your photos done

531.

The photo of the farmer's field looks like it's been cropped

532.

I have hundreds of videos of people's toes. I really have a lot of footage.

533.

I'm trying to research adverts for skips online but whenever I click on 'Skip Ad' a music video starts up

534.

Rod Hull always carried with him an electronic device which made kitten noises. It annoyed everyone else but he wouldn't part with his e-mew.

535.

I received an email telling me how to read maps backwards but I already knew it would be spam

536.

My browser asked me if I wanted to open another window and I thought, yes, it is getting quite stuffy in here

537.

My kids think 'I Claudius' is some sort of Apple product, in Times New Roman

538.

Elon Musk has backed down and said I can take my pet seabird into space - for a suitable payment. Well that's a tern up for the bucks.

One of my professional connections suggested we keep in touch using two empty baked bean cans connected by a piece of string. I said, "Mate, I can't believe anyone still uses Link Tin!"

540.

For one of my recent courier jobs I had to deliver a data storage device to a village high in the Alps. That was a hard drive.

541.

I'VE REALLY PUT IN A SHIFT TODAY

542.

I'm getting sick of people posting gluten-free recipes on Twitter. Maybe I'm developing a t'weet intolerance.

THE PAST

History

543.

The Eternal City could only afford to pay its contract workmen because Rome wasn't billed in a day

544.

Medieval knights first fought with spades, before they developed a proper code off shovelry

545.

Anyone erecting an inflatable neolithic monument must be unhenged

546.

Sir Lancelot's biggest fear was sitting on his sewing kit in the dark. He was terrified of anything which would go bum pin the knight.

547.

In 1215 the barons demanded that King John agree to clear up after the volcanic eruption at Runnymede and that's how they got their Magma Carter

548.

It's almost 200 years since William 'Buffalo Bill' Cody was born. I'm looking forward to his bisontenary.

549.

By keeping the side dish separate from his main course Emporer Hadrian became the first known person to have a Walled-off Salad

550.

In 1588, the lookout who spotted the Spanish ships arriving off the coast of England was charged with deserting his post for shouting: "Armada here!"

Nostalgia

551.

My best friend at school said his dad worked for Bontempi.
I didn't know what that was, but they were good times.

552.

Just dug up the stones under the old railway line I worked
on years ago. That was a ballast from the past.

553.

I remember when Botham was England captain, the
Reverend Paisley was NI leader, and IDS was the Tory
leader - but that all seems like Ians ago

THE SEA

Fish

554.

I got my fussy child to eat the seafood at our Spanish holiday home. I'm pleased with our plaice in the son.

555.

I was fishing at the riverbank and a passer-by told me my flies were down. I said, "It's not a surprise - they're soon going to be eaten by fish."

556.

My pet monkfish likes his routine. He's a creature of habit.

557.

- That shark looks huge. Is it Jaws?

- No, it's somebody else's

558.

As I watched Jamie Oliver serve up fish with tartare sauce, I saw something small and green in it. I thought, this is going to be another one of his capers.

559.

The wife says I don't listen and wishes I'd get a fish disease. Well I am not getting herring aids.

560.

- I've just tricked a Swedish sailor out of his life savings

- Scammed a Navy 'un?

- Yeah, I told you, he's Swedish?!

561.

I seem to have mislaid my small volcanic island. Have you seen it atoll?

562.

Do electric eels think it's great to be a live?

563.

I felt so enthusiastic on the first day of my scuba diving course but they told me not to jump in feet first

564.

I'm thrilled to know my phone call to the Sea Life Centre may be used for training and monitoring porpoises

565.

I've just been offered a contract measuring the depth of sea channels. It's rather a plumb job.

566.

Just how could Moses part the waters of the Red Sea, God dam it?!

567.

To capture all those whales swimming in formation on Blue Planet, it must have been orcastrated

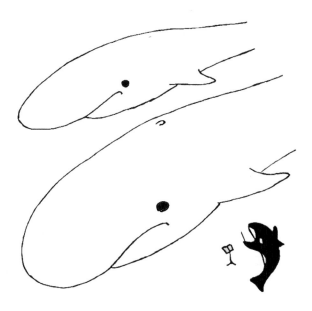

568.

I'm feeling rather subdued - like the cool guy on a U-Boat

569.

We all live in a yellow submarine, even though my tenancy
agreement says I'm not allowed to sublet

570.

I heard rumours there would be a place to park my U-Boat
at the harbour but it turned out they had no sub stance

TV & FILM

Cartoons

571.

My old Looney Tunes app still has Bugs in it

572.

Tweetypie imagined he could stop Sylvester by reading Huckleberry Finn to him but that was a ridiculous Twain of Thwart

573.

Did the film TinTin come with canned laughter?

574.

My ready meal said 'Cook from Frozen', and I thought....... "I don't remember that character in the film."

575.

My wife woke me up today with a bout of slapping across the back of my neck. I forgive her though. I love the spell of nape palm in the morning.

576.

If you think the guy who crossed the Alps with elephants was bad you need a Hannibal lecture

577.

I just watched a crow in a British comedy film. What a carrion.

578.

- Many films with characters played by Michael Caine happen to be banned in Indonesia

- Including Jakarta?

- Yes, they don't like the violent gangsters

579.

No-one can win the Cannes Film Festival's main prize any more as it's been stolen by prostitutes. Organisers are to step up security but they're simply closing the Palme d'Or after the whores have bolted.

580.

The Hollywood director with the worst personal hygiene was Alfred Itchcock

581.

I know this is overly soppy but I think I've fallen for the lady at work who compiles and analyses statistics and uses them to calculate insurance rates and premiums. It's Love, Actuary.

582.

Many handguns were made and used by T-Rex's at Jurassic Park. No-one could stop those small arms manufacturers.

583.

Any librarians who insist on doing Sir Sean Connery
impressions, I say, get over your shelves

584.

James Bond is getting older and now has to wear glasses.
The next Bond film will be called 'Your four eyes only'.

585.

Roger Moore once dropped in on my local takeaway and
of course they gave him favourable treatment. They made
him a special curry sauce and said it's "For your rice only."

TV Programmes

586.

In this year's 'Animals Got Talent' final, the sheep performing in a playground got the people's vote. They had a big swing and won by a lamb slide.

587.

When Lee Majors heard there were imminent auditions for the part of the Six Million Dollar Man he knew he had to act fast

588.

There was a 70's TV series where I thought the forensic pathologist's mouth was going to be an important part of the plot but it was just Quincy dental

589.

ITV's new entertainment show Sailors Got Talent could be a ratings disaster

590.

After poor ratings, the BBC's Springwatch programme is to move to ITV and be rebranded 'Bitterns Got Talons'

THE UNITED KINGDOM

England

591.

- I'm travelling to Hertfordshire tomorrow

- Hitchin?

- No, I'll probably just drive

592.

They say you can take the man out of Manchester but those left behind would then be in Chester

593.

My favourite English county is Kent. Sorry, not Surrey.

594.

With my good contacts in Hertfordshire I've been asked to represent one of their towns at the Garden City awards. I'm Welwyn.

595.

This year's noisiest resort award went to Klaxon-on-Sea

596.

I just watched a drama about Beachy Head. It was quite edgy.

597.

My wife has handed me a one-way ticket to Norfolk. There's no coming back from Diss.

598.

- I've just discovered Spielberg's living in the same New Town as me in Hertfordshire!

- Stevenage?

- I reckon he must be in his 70's

Scotland

599.

I spent Burns Night in Stockholm enjoying a swede dish meal

600.

My new girlfriend's ex keeps threatening to take her and jump off the Forth Bridge. Why cantilever alone?

601.

My Scottish mate's takeaway business wasn't liked in England. He said, "They may take our rice, but they never take our free dim sum".

602.

When I lived in Edinburgh I enquired about tattoo removal but they just stayed on, parading every night right up until the end of August

603.

I've brought you back more than one bottle from Tobermory - in fact, Mull tipple ones

WEARABLES

Clothes

604.

I'm wearing pirated foil underwear - I'm in Long John's Silver

605.

"We are all a product of our jeans" - Levi Strauss

606.

I like to wrestle wearing large trousers stuffed with dried grass. They call me 'Giant hay slacks'.

607.

I was excited to find some Bucks Fizz memorabilia for sale but they were asking five grand for Cheryl's skirt which was a rip off!

608.

I studded hard to be a punk rocker

609.

[At hotel check-in desk]

- So, what do you need from me?

- Just your name and address

- Well, it's Richard Pulsford. And here's a lovely flowery frock which no longer fits me.

610.

I like Elizabethan clothing and Scientology. But then, who isn't into some ruff sects?

Perfume

611.

The strength of eau de cologne is measured per fume

612.

Before Shakespeare's playwriting took off he was a door-to-door perfume salesman but was sacked for stealing the products and he could never shake off his reputation as being barred from Avon

613.

The longest railway tunnel in the world is the Gotthard Base Tunnel in Switzerland, but by far the most fragrant one is the Chanel Tunnel

WORDS

Dyslexia

614.

Because of my dyslexia I can never get through to the Marmite and Coastguard Agency

615.

Thanks to my dyslexia I had to get the baking instructions for meringue read out to me line by line. What a pavlova.

616.

I have to look up Jacob Rees-Mogg's use of slang in the
Urbane Dictionary

617.

Saying 'Pret' is just a little Pretentious

618.

I found my missing pocket dictionary in my jeans when I
unloaded the washing machine. There are no words.

619.

You can talk blue without speaking - just use cyan
language

620.

So what if I enjoy playing with the meaning of words? It's
just some antics.

621.

I said, "I promise I'll stop my habit of thinking up lists of words for jokes."

He said, "Famous last words?"

So I said, "Post, Orders, Resort, Rites, Chance Saloon, Man Standing, Hurrah, Laugh, Gasp, Straw, Lap, Legs, Judgement, Supper, Christmas..."

622.

I'm writing a novel about hens. It's a story with many layers.

623.

It took me a while to get into writing real thigh-slapping jokes but now I'm finally hitting my strides

624.

I'm writing a sitcom about 3 hard-up accident-prone farmers who use their all-terrain vehicle to sell off their remaining pigs. It's called 'Last of the Hummer Swine'.

625.

I don't know what you call a small spillage from a pen but I have an inkling

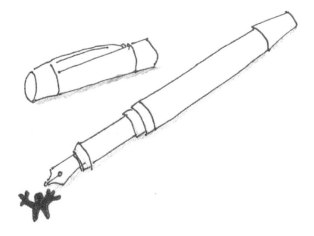

WORK

Companies

626.

I see Fiat is going to merge with Tesco. It will either be a Fiasco or they'll make a Teat of themselves.

627.

My mate thinks Naomi Campbell should be the new face of Greggs but is she really the best roll model?

628.

Apple must make a huge turnover

629.

I asked BT if I could have a shorter number and they said no.

630.

I don't like the way Royal Mail think they're better than the Stobart Group, driving round with their 'haulier than thou' attitude

631.

I hated working in the storage depot. One day, I had to eat all the wood the goods were held on. It was all so unpalletable.

632.

I got sacked from my job at Citroen when they found out I'd been lying on my 2cv

633.

After I'd botched a job trimming the hedges on an estate, the owners took me in for questioning. It was good copse, bad copse.

634.

It suited me being a supervisor in the overall factory

635.

I'm a wreck. My boss has asked me for all of last year's figures by tomorrow and I think it's touch and go whether I'll have a breakdown before then.

636.

Rather than retire I'm going to go part-time with the glove puppetry as I reckon it's good to keep your hand in

637.

All these loudspeaker announcements at work, do they just do it tannoy?

638.

I don't like work's clear desk policy because I can see my thighs through it

639.

I used to work as a swimming pool attendant but it wasn't interesting - after a spate of children's 'accidents' in the pool it felt like I was always just going through the motions

Printed in Great Britain
by Amazon